THOUGHTS OF A MADMAN PART 2

THOUGHTS OF A MADMAN PART 2

BY: ANTHONY STAFFORD

Seed Royale Publishing

CONTENTS

It's only one thing in life that is promised to of and this is death even though we know that day will come losing the ones you love the most is never easy. To my beloved Aunty's Cil and Savonia, I thank you for all the love you gave and for always believing in me. You loved me through my rights and wrongs knowing I would do better I love y'all forever.

Photo By:
Anthony Stafford

The first time I ever wrote a poem is when I learned of the death of my mother's twin sister on the morning of they 45 birthday which became page five of my first book the Thoughts of A Madman. This outlet gave me a way to channel these thoughts in a beneficial way you can't control your thoughts but you have control on how you act on them. I'm 36 years old, 2 times convicted of a felony, father of 8 the owner of

two LLC companies and the owner of properties saying this to show
that anything is possible as long as you put your mind to it.

Abu Mumia Jamal

In 2011 I was sent to a SCI, now myself not being from PA
it was all new to me being 24 at the time. They moved me
into a cell and about two months later they told my cellie
and I we would have to move to another cell because they
was making it a single cell from a prisoner just getting off
death row.
A few days later he walks on the housing unit he was a
older guy, brown skin wore glasses and had dreads you
could see his hair was receding he looked like a Rasta.
Everyone started to flock around him like groupies, again
he just looked like a person who didn't even belong there
soft spoken and laid back everyone kept saying his name
Mumia. This Mumia, our first encounter we was in the
chow hall for lunch and he was sitting right across from
me and I asked him was he Rasta he told me no he was
apart of MOVE an African Movement. So one day I was
watching Law and Order and they said his name on the
show I was like wow, soon as the doors opened I went
right to him and was like they were talking about you on
Law and Order. Then listened to a song by Tupac mention-
ing him, another song by Beanie Sigel mentioned him. I
told him he was so shocked he wanted to hear it. But still
the most humble man and very approachable, told him
about a dream I had of him walking out of there in a suit.
His remark was very funny. Even gave me tips on writing.
To the brother Abu Mumia Jamal much love.
To the woman of the world:

Photo By:

Anthony Stafford

Photo By:

Anthony Stafford

I'm no sexist my actions and behavior to the opposite sex was horrible and very shameful. My self living in a man body but still with thoughts of a child and I didn't fully understand the importance of the woman in my life. I truly believe that a strong woman is the foundation and backbone of that of her partner. Again all women are strong some realize it sooner than others but when they find themselves they understand it. It very much shows they carry the weight of others for months. I love you Mommy, Aunties Grandmothers, Sisters and all the women of the world.

CHAPTER 1

The Mind

The mind through conventional wisdom would say "You can't control the thoughts that come into your head". In actuality, this proclamation is not entirely an untruth for the only thing we can control is how we act on those thoughts intrusive or otherwise.

Hope, fear, love, evil, good, bad, what are these things to the richest or poorest in society?
We all have our ups and downs it shows & is evident even with the rich or affluent a person can and will still take his or her own very life. Someone exposed to the bad doesn't always want to do good or be virtuous when it is so easy to do wrong.

Even when you know something is inherently wrong you are left fighting every demon in your body to live right. To quote a line from 50 Cent's song " I'm supposed to die tonight"
I don't know if I'm GOD'S child/
or Satan's Angel/.
Still,
I have so much love in my heart and can only hope for the best things to come.

Photo By:
Anthony Stafford

CHAPTER 2

A Feeling of Pain

A feeling of pain and a feeling of self defeat brings you down to the point where your mind and body find it difficult to function. You don't want to move, it feels as if you're having a heart attack everything in your body feels as though it is shutting down.

The love you have for a person, for life, for something greater than yourself, drives you to do your best & be your best. It gives you an overwhelming feeling of being wanted & accepted as well as confidence in the notion that you will find a person that gives you that matching drive in your life.

To win is often rare, we often celebrate our small wins big, so finding that person to love you for who you are, not only for what you can do for them, is nothing short of miraculous if not amazing.

CHAPTER 3

Love of Religion

Where did this word love come from? Who put the meaning to this four letter word that is so powerful but sometimes used in meaningless ways to hurt & kill others over its power.

I believed in religion even with many doubts & many unanswered questions, but hoped through faith that I was doing what was right. It's safe to say that this belief brought me nothing but fear & depression. To be brutally honest with so many religions to choose from how does anyone really know which one is right.?

A Jewish man may be a devout believer, lives his everyday life by the Torah following the laws wholeheartedly. He may even help those outside of his community. He gives because he knows it's the right moral thing to do, again based on his beliefs.

Then you have a woman born a Christian, raised in the church who misses little or no services & pays all offerings and tithes, even when her bills are dangerously late. In faith, she leaves everything in God's hands. Her trust is only in the word of God. You have a husband and wife that live their everyday life in accordance to the Islamic law respecting all. The thing is, with four righteous people only one will make it to heaven according to their beliefs. Is this a fair assessment?

There is a man who wears a Pennant, dresses in all black & loves the serpents, but this is what he does in his spare time. He is an owner of a nonprofit that helps homeless and battered woman. He never talks about his beliefs nor does he share them with anyone. Then a cruel fate, as a photo of him is spread & goes viral on the internet. Now this "Great Man" is considered the most evil, vile person the town has ever laid eyes on. How did this perception of him change so drastically?

CHAPTER 4

God is...

Who is and what is God? Is God Jesus or is he the Son of God? How can the father be the son and the son be the father? I pray my son learns from my mistakes and is nothing like me or to put it better, be a more evolved version of me. I can share my shortcomings with him and teach him things through my own experience. I can show him where I went wrong & came up short. In teaching him these things, I honor not only myself but also God.

I ask God why? as I lay here in my bed stomach hurting from hunger, cold, wondering why I can only see a Christmas gift from the TV? & can only imagine what a Wonderful Thanksgiving dinner may smell like.

CHAPTER 5

Opinions on Life

What is losing ? What is a loss? As long as there is still life there is a chance of winning. We can not give up learning from our mistakes & mishaps for this is what truly shapes us.

How do you hate a person you never met because of an opinion placed in your head by someone else? Unaware of what is behind the dislike of this person. Is this not a commitment to ignorance in a nutshell?

Recently I watched a really good show. Actually, It was a movie about Love. You always know when it's real because when you are watching TV or a movie, you're watching someone else's creative thoughts, so the idea of love is still out there and the same thing applies with the bad.

CHAPTER 6

It's Tricky

They say the best trick the devil ever played on us was making us believe he didn't exist. How many times has a person not believed the truth that was right in front of them? I mean right in black in white.

As I laid in bed, deep in my thoughts I didn't know where to start. I had mixed feelings about everything. At times it feels like everything I was taught growing up was all just a huge lie. Could it be a message that I have to look inside deep to figure things out? (It sounds cliche I know) but they say everything happens for a reason.

They say that family is everything. But oftentimes those are your worst enemies. Sometimes they are the ones that want to see you fall. It's frustrating because they'll support those with no kinship but pray for the demise of a person sharing their own bloodline, the Cain and Abel effect you feel me?

CHAPTER 7

Love or Lust

Love or Lust. The beauty is caught by the eyes which then proceed to send a signal to the brain, more than often corrupting the heart. Love or Lust following deep infatuation with a image.

  As she walks into the bar her short skirt & bright red lipstick turn every head. Her light brown eyes & jet black hair sit right down next to her target. He could see her & the sweet smell of her perfume caught his attention, he is sexually aroused. They make eye contact one thing leads to another, one shot of Hennessy and a line of coke & it was all she wrote. Safe to assume that condom he left in his wallet had no chance. She was already on him like he was a horse and she was the knight. When she was done they didn't even exchange names or numbers, this was her, get back to the man that gave it to her.

I know my wife loves me and I tell her that I love her all the time. The problem is every time I leave the house I'm cheating on her as if I'm living a crazy double life. I come home hop in the shower, kiss her and that is when the thought runs
through my head: What if she is doing the same thing to me? Paranoid, I check her phone,
pick fights with her (God knows I'm dead wrong) I attack her trying to cover up my own demons when she has devoted her entire life to me and our family. Somehow, I make her feel as if she's doing some-thing wrong.

Perfection. What is being perfect? Can something or someone be truly perfect? What I see and how my brain processes this sight that captures my heart brings tears to my eyes & gives me hope. Another person may walk up & laugh in my face & think this whole thing is a waste of time what a piece of junk. But it stands,
Beauty is in the eye of the Beholder.

CHAPTER 8

Upbringing

Photo By:
Anthony Stafford

You grow up taught to live by a very strict code, a part of a brotherhood, a gang whatever you want to call it and everyone wants to lead with no clue where to start but everyone can't be a boss. The blind leading the blind, this code gets you life in jail, set up, and told on by your leader. One simple reason he was in love with your wife and was jealous of your life.

I was born 1986 Newark, NJ my Mother was 18 years old, Father 21, you can't as a unborn child understand what life you going to take on. You don't choose what family you will be born into. You're not born knowing pain or what's rich or poor. You are not born understanding hate, only what you will be taught and exposed to in the most important years of your upbringing.

You have no religion so you don't believe in Heaven or what they say is Hell but when this is described to you a paradise can be created on Earth as well in Hell. Think of a person in jail, every morning he or she wakes up to be reminded of all their wrongs no matter how much they repent they can't (seem) to make it right. Then for a person that has everything this world has to offer, it could be the greatest gift to a person who never had anything.

Hi my friend you think you could get rid of me so easily by sharing your thoughts? Come on Depression just leave me alone. What more do you want from me? Boy you better stop before I call my boy Anxiety he got the biggest personality disorder so you can't shake me off that fast. Look Depression, I do what you ask I just share with you whether it's good or bad I just hope it helps someone understand they not alone. Then you send Anxiety to attack me, crippling me, bringing me down to my knees. I expect you both the good and the bad.

I was raised in the church every Friday and Sunday I was at a service spending a lot of time with my Grandmother and Poppy my Father's parents. My Grandfather, who i called Poppy, was a Pastor who married my Grandma when my Dad was 10 years old. I believe they was 36 years old when I was born. Just moving to a house they now own in East Orange NJ.

Photo By:
Anthony Stafford

CHAPTER 9

Through a Child's Eyes

Certain times when we're kids, I worried when I shouldn't have had a care in the world. Understanding things I was exposed to, processing them in my mind the way I could understand. At a young age I developed a real level of anger, to the point when the tears started to flow. I would lose all control, only wanting to bring the same feeling to the person or thing that brought these tears to my eyes. I understood every bible story I was ever told and knowing the good goes to Heaven and the bad goes to Hell, created a fear every night. I felt the Devil had a hold on me sometimes dreaming of being held down in a place what they described as Hell.

I was only a kid still in grade school when I was bullied because I had less than others. Often jumped by the other kids in the neighborhood. I had no one to protect me from the older kids.

Photo By:
Anthony Stafford

My Mother had myself and two other kids. My Brother and I are 18 months apart & I believe now being an older Brother, & protector, I have to make sure what I go through or went through stays away from them.

My Mother's Father and Mother, I spent a lot of time with them growing up. I'm blessed to have all my Grandparents. Both of my Grandfathers served in the US Military. My Mother's Father died when I was 6, so the first time I was introduced to death was from a person that gave me hope and believed I would be something some day.

Now as a kid losing someone so close, it hurts so bad that you guard yourself from feelings and getting attached because no matter how hard you cry you can't see them again, you only hear that they are in heaven.

I was introduced to death, my Mother being a young woman, took it hard and turned to the streets. I started school in the First Grade, so I was behind in all my lessons, so I was made fun of. The oldest, so I got picked on by the other kids. I had no protection turned to anger and developed rage, they became my two best friends. Still trying to hold on to all the bible stories I was told as kid.

I'm not a trouble maker I don't look for problems. I'm not a bully I'm keeping up with everyone else around me, always been big for my age so I had to take on bigger kids. You can't run home getting Mommy. Mommy going to get you for running, stand there and fight. Now placed in an all boys class Special Education for Learning and Behavior Issues seeing a doctor trying to figure out why I am the way I am.

I've seen the house with no food, the lights cut off, no clean clothes, holidays was only enjoyed from watching TV. My brother and I 6-7 washing car windows to help put food in the house. Lived around drugs, seen guns, been into a lot of fights, seen my Mother abused, tasted death, all before the age of 10 years old. My first pet was a roach.

CHAPTER 10

In Retrospect

How could you judge me when your only access to me is a file that was also prepared by a person who doesn't even know me? Your feelings of who I am is biased & based off of a textbook from a degree you were given to "properly" understand me.

I'm older now (finding other religion's) but the fear of not going to church stops you from learning about other things, because it's sending you a one way trip to Hell. Introduced to now playing football, no more church on Sunday's, I began to hate church because the people there was so judgmental, as if they looked down on you. One I'm a bastard born out of wedlock, my mean streak people think something is wrong with me. As i got older, I began to fight back with my Mother all the things they say you shouldn't do in the bible.

Now, I'm introduced to gangs. Never really was a person to follow, only plans was to be a respected leader, no more wanting to be a Cop, Firefighter. The feeling of love and doing right was now gone. Taking no matter if I was right always found myself in the wrong. Still had the hope from my Poppy but that also too faded away.

How do I believe in books that have been proven to be false? Bending you to control and kill others, ruin lives? How do I believe in this if I don't believe I'm going to Hell and not believing in what my family taught me. I will be in Hell, while they live in Heaven.

Pain, Pain it's giving me everything overcoming, all that has come my way even when I wanted to give up, pain wouldn't let me. When I took all the sleeping pills and wrapped a sheet around my neck, pain. To understand the good, to love and expect the good, to enjoy the good, you have to know the bad. I can't complain about life because I do believe in destiny and that everything happened the way it was supposed to.

I was raised by a women that had 6 kids. Me as the oldest, that struggled and went through everything with her as she grew in life, but did the best she could. This woman would always tell me if you can't respect your Mother you would never be able to love or treat a woman right. Now my name is in that of statistics of Domestic Violence.

Spending time in jail, for years forced me to look at myself. All my actions, wrongdoings, taking the blame putting it on me. I can't blame my family, they loved me the best they knew how. We all humans and we grow and learn together. I held all my emotion, all my feelings, but one thing that saved me is the thought of love. The biggest love of my children. Whoever I knew that loved me, loved the thought of who they thought I was and that they could change me, not for who I was, what I been through. This doesn't apply for all, I was blessed to have some of the best kid's mothers, 6 daughters and 2 sons.

Photo By:
Anthony Stafford

Photo By:
Anthony Stafford

Even in jail my body was controlled but I'm a thinker putting together a master plan, understanding me, my wrongs, 5 years later two LLC companies, home owner, writer and whatever else I put my mind to it's all about the thought that you put into action and taking your place in the world that is meant for you. A Mother always in my eyes knows best and My

Mother was always right even when I didn't want to see it.

The moral of story is:

Never give up, care less of what others have, just focus on what you want. Plan how to get it and be the best YOU that YOU can be. People will try to figure you out, but only leave them with a trail of good actions. We are human so it is suffice to say we will make some mistakes, hell a lot of mistakes, but that is all part of life. The wealthiest people are those who are some of the biggest risk takers. But if you ask me what I believe, I tell you this,

I believe in the Power of Love and within that Love there is an empathy and a Greatness for all

Photo By:
Anthony Stafford

"In the darkness I see the light through my tears I see so clearly I can't hide my pain

I don't want to not question anything that has been put in my life.

In my heart I feel discomfort walking around with the Devil on my shoulder.

Everyday is a learning experience whether it's good or it's bad I continue to do my best.

I don't blame no one for my misfortunes in love and couldn't have asked for a better Mother whose

strength and courage shaped me to be the person I am today." -Anthony Stafford

Photo By:
Anthony Stafford

Anthony Stafford was born in Newark, NJ he's the oldest of 6 kids.
He started playing football at the age of 10 for the East Orange Rams
& wrestled in Middle School. In College he won his first gold medal for Wrestling at his Community College Wrestling Club.
In 2016 he released his critically acclaimed debut book
"Thoughts of a Madman" to rave reviews.
   In his spare time,Anthony raises and breeds snakes for his YouTube channel called "Madman Serpents".

Photo By:
Anthony Stafford

A family man, Anthony has 6 daughters and two sons, with a grandchild on the way.

"I grew up shy and used violence as a way to express myself.
It wasn't until my Aunt's death did I begin to actually express myself through writing."

Anthony owns Prime Time Lawn Service LLC and Stafford Trucking LLC. He also manages artists through his company Big Backing Entertainment as well as provides security at Catch 22 Club in Allentown, Pa.
Special Shout outs to:
Billy king CMR
Bill Felony BBE/MDG

Dex Hillsek BBE/Hillsek studio
8 squad rebel Radio
Baby Boy Beast mode Entertainment
Goouch Select few
Urban city reptiles

Big backin entertainment presen

PICTURES

O. T.

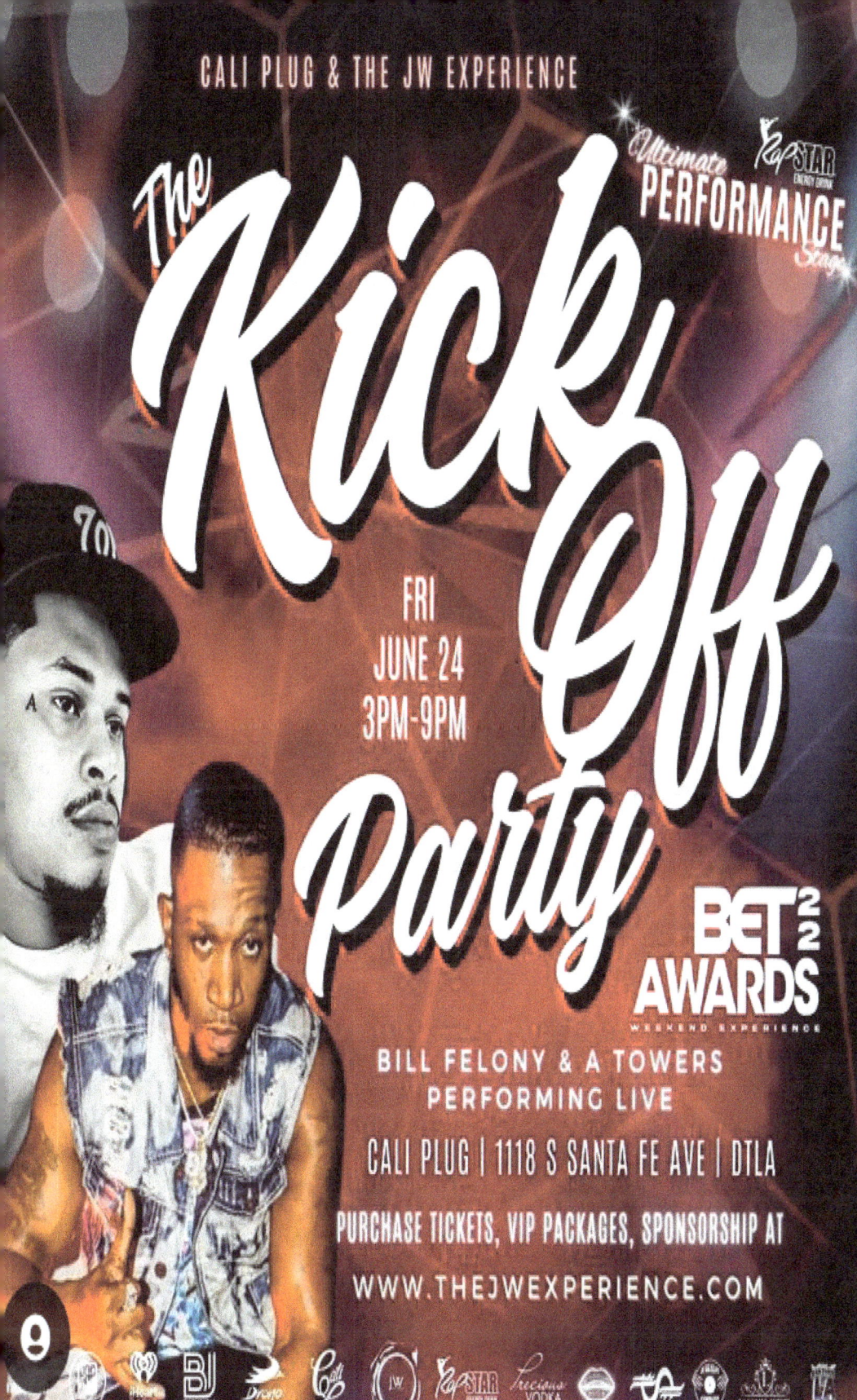

PICTURES

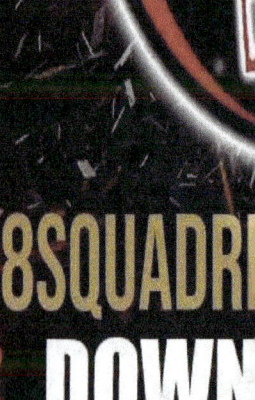

ATEVER GOES
DIO PODCAST

8SQUADRI

DOWN
OUR

RDAY 10PM - 12AM

Get ya tickets B4 dey sold out

BILL FELONY
ALBUM RELEASE PARTY
JUNE 10TH 2022

This friday

$25 TICKETS

LUCKY
SPECIAL GUEST ARTIST

DJ SCOOBY RU

DOOR OPENS 7PM
SHOW STARTS 10PM
BROADCAST LIVE 11PM

HOSTED BY CHECKMATED RYDERZ MANAGEMENT LLC
617A CENTRAL AVENUE EAST ORANGE NEW JERSEY

No.071

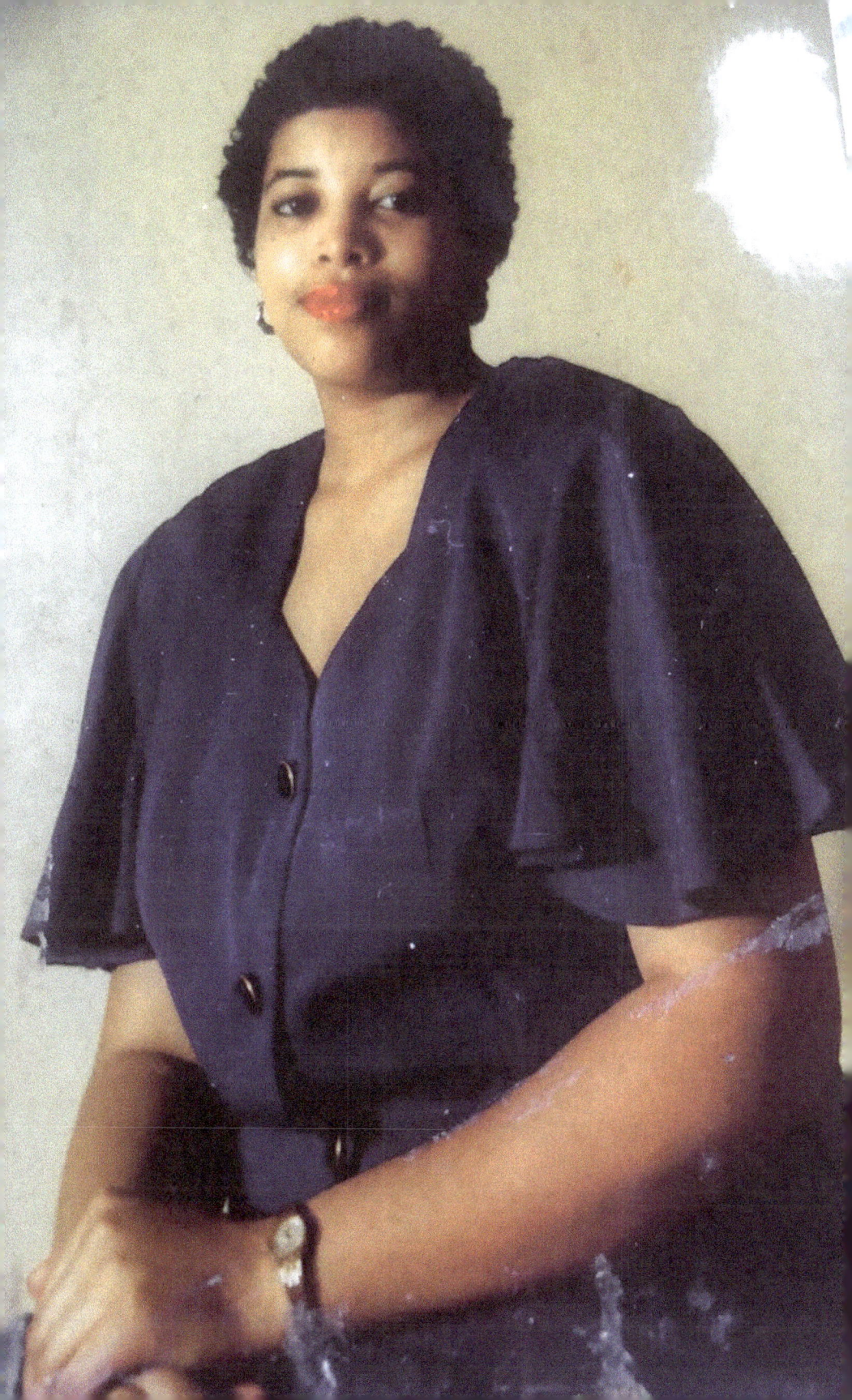

BBE & MDG

PRESENTS

FREESTYLE
CYPHER TAKEOVER

ON SPECIAL GUEST FRIDAY

12TH AUGUST ● 10PM-12AM

BILL FELONY **MZ QUALITY** **DEX HILLSEK** **NISAF BABY**

SPECIAL INVITED GUEST

SUBSCRIBE TO YOUTUBE OR TWITCH APP: 8 SQUAD REBEL RADIO TV

SPONSORED BY CHECKMATE RYDERZ MANAGEMENT LLC

HOSTED BY KING CHECKMATE

Party bus 2013

2016/0

SQUAD REBEL

RADIO

www.ingramcontent.com/pod-product-compliance
Lightning Source LLC
Chambersburg PA
CBHW060354130626
46553CB00003B/1230